T0170847

THRONG

Jose Perez Beduya

Lake Forest College Press

Lake Forest

First published 2012 by &NOW Books, an imprint of Lake Forest College Press.

Carnegie Hall
Lake Forest College
555 N. Sheridan Road
Lake Forest, IL 60045

lakeforest.edu/andnow

Cover photos by Poklong Anading

Lake Forest College Press publishes in the broad spaces of Chicago studies. Our imprint, &NOW Books, publishes innovative and conceptual literature and serves as the publishing arm of the &NOW writers' conference and organization.

ISBN: 978-0-9823156-7-5
ISSN: 0-9823156-7-8

Book design by Vasiliki Gerentes

Printed in the United States

For my parents
and for Jessica

CONTENTS

FOREWORD

Jose Perez Beduya's *Throng* thoughtfully layers aesthetic, political, and spiritual registers into a subtly moving whole. At the heart of this remarkable debut stands a *we* that emits a vital human signal, despite being adrift in a suburban-technological labyrinth as dehumanizing as George Oppen's corporate city "Glassed / In dreams." Against an ever-present authoritarian backdrop, Beduya's "Tenderized / Post-citizens" buoy identity with defiant acts of imagination and mimesis. Like the people who make up this *we*, the poems in *Throng* support each other. This is truly a unified *work*, and deserves to be read as such.

Beduya has structured *Throng* around two repeated sequences, "Morrow" and "Inside the Bright Wheel." The first is often painterly and concerned with art and futurity, "We wanted to record / the rain faithfully"; the second, a series of short hinge-like poems, gives witness to the deceptive nature of cordoned-off spaces and too-easy stories. There are "warm and scented breezes" inside the Bright Wheel, but when you look closer there is also the "skin and knotted hair of strangers." It is a place where the "poor are still poor," a place of amnesia, but also the "bosom of the law." One thinks of an over-lit twenty-first century mall, or, the veneer of comforts we cling to in the heart of capitalism. By the end of the book the Bright Wheel becomes quite oppressive, the difference between *inside* and *outside* erased: "In veined light / Our prisoners' torsos / Minus electrodes / Mirror ours."

The mirror is a repeated motif, symbolizing mimesis as a necessary, if deceptive, device used to shape identity. Mirrors are masks: "We are known by mirrors," and we must "mass-produce / Mirrors to stay what we are." Imaginative and aesthetic escapes are strangled by the tentacles of state power until, "All we are / Are our papers." The contrast between these two incompatible ways of knowing is starkly represented in the poem "Autumn Evening": "And when she lies down / For a long time in the field / Attempting to decipher / The temperamental night sky / Sees the long swords / Of flashlights approaching." This scene of star-gazing interrupted by police flashlights positions the state as a barrier between humans and nature where "By spinning cop-light / We are found / Roaming in our sleepwear"; later such moments will be ominously combined into a "Tree of teargas and truncheons."

The relationship of Beduya's *we* to the lyric *I* is made explicit in one of his "Morrow" poems through a vivid image that recalls Elizabeth Bishop's "The Weed": "I reach deep inside / Myself and extract / People now living in tents / There is no end to them . . ." This is surrealist picture-making in the service of psychic multiplicity; the artist's self is invaded by his insistent *we*, he cannot disconnect, nor forget the way a people's spirit of rebellion can be pacified through mechanization: "We began as daggers / Later made neutral / Later made cogs." This process extends to the global technocracy, as chillingly depicted in "The Fuse," a poem in which our faces shake "violently in the mornings" until steadied by "soft clicks" and "bright screens."

Yet amidst state surveillance and dehumanized landscapes, amidst the *throng*, Beduya plants a pair of human hands, literally: "we buried // Our hands in the hard soil." Reminiscent of Keats's *living hand*, reaching toward us from beyond the grave, Beduya's hands come to represent both the *making* that is art, "Sometimes our hands / were their own people," and the *imaginative* connection to a higher power: "How do we / Extinguish our hands / in prayer." Unlike the faces in *Throng*, which are "voted most mask-like," the hands are authentic. They carry the residue of human gesture, the crucial somatic element: "If you must take my life / Spare these hands."

The poems in *Throng* guide us with a subtle music that belies the complexity of their content. To quote from the cryptic and wonderful poem, "Book X," *Throng* is a "diagram of pure thinking."

Jennifer Moxley, Judge
2011-2012 Madeleine P. Plonsker
Emerging Writer's Residency Prize

THRONG

THE SEARCH PARTY

In the fields
We were boys

And girls finding debris
Gathering notes

With nothing to report
A people very inside ourselves

We found each other
Through a system of ropes and smells

Our long, stumbling days
Began and ended

With ballad versions of the prayers
We were taught in different tongues

Flashes and rustling
From copying machines replaced

Our voices when they failed
The images we've tucked under rocks

Scattered with the wind
That moves all merchandise

Guarding against numbness
We started small fires

Everywhere we went
Only when we buried

Our hands in the hard soil
Of the valley

Did the throbbing surrounding
Hills become a part of us

BOOK X

Taking pictures
Less and less
We dream with a train
Behind our heads
And light leaking everywhere
Undefeated
The news is gray
From the labyrinth
And when the neon fog crawls in
We remember our place
By the sound of our neighbor's
Children coughing
In this grid
Where one weak
Lullaby ends
Is where another
Galloping away begins
Day aches but
Sleep also aches
Across the sky unfolds
A diagram of pure thinking
It is as far away as it is fast
And coming to save us
We christen it Beautiful Insect
We kill it with our eyelids

AUTUMN EVENING

Who can keep meat the longest
In his mouth without laughing
Or weeping wins a prize
Who slows the video down enough
Watches bricks smudge
The sides of heads
Who leaves
The train at the border
Arrives at the same moment
Via bullet wound
Who lives alone
Will be surrounded by armless angels
And when she lies down
For a long time in the field
Attempting to decipher
The temperamental night sky
Sees the long swords
Of flashlights approaching
Who looks on calmly at the conflagration
Thinks of the city from a shrine

MORROW

With each of us
Paired lifelong
To an object we perfected
After countless
Precise repeats
We misplaced the meaning
Of what we did
But discovered a new cleanliness
And let empty rooms
Rush over us
Sometimes our hands
Were their own people
In the squares
Tearing bread
Holding and letting
Go of flocks
We kept drinking
The medicine of another day
Imagining the sunlight
Were gloved hands reaching down
Through a hole in the century
To anesthetize us
Although we were very
Far away in our thoughts
We always came back
To our neighbors
Their wives
And our landlords
We felt the spirit to be
Near but also displaced
Waiting in dreams
Watching spit freeze

PARTS

Alone in a night garden saying

        I am I am

        This empire   butchers   choirs

Its errors
            Displayed as green rooms
      Later made raw

Hills in post-production

        The shepherds there are sediment

While inside you, my absentee,
        Snow dead pixels

To your nightgown sticks Welcome
        Back to the Show

            Heart playing its one red loop louder

        In your skull as the music
More tightly strangles you

The music swelling
            Begins to fail

        The host is on his knees again

The crowd refrains
            From laughter

            For laughter has many holes

Standing so still to listen to each other

            We make a dull ringing sound

INSIDE THE BRIGHT WHEEL

Are warm and scented breezes
But we soon discover
The skin and knotted hair of strangers

INSIDE THE BRIGHT WHEEL

Is a looped reel of the founding
Of our island nation
Intercuttings of protests
And political sermons

INSIDE THE BRIGHT WHEEL

We tremble and kiss
We lie down in riot fields

INSIDE THE BRIGHT WHEEL

Shivering you sit
At one end of a see-saw
While the vast and buzzing
Night
A factory
And all-seeing
God sit opposite

STATIONS

The blinding of the masters
After the showing of the instruments.

Cut to a piano from an oval
Window being played.

And then I test my throat
In the gated community.

Segue to a change
Of person but exactly

The same scenery.
On helmet cam

The night twittering
And its saddest guards.

Summer ghost,
When I stand behind your dress

I see deeply inside my face.
These arms live

Separately and far away.
They feed

Words back to my house
Where my plaster torso waits

All day at the writing desk
Inside a hospital gown

While the radio announces
Under a snow

Of stadium seats the police
Is finally married to the crowds.

BREATHING EXERCISES

No sleep

No standing against
The horizon line

No harm

No knees

No coming to an end

No quickness

No razor wire

No little boy
Digging with a spoon to open
An ocean this far into the shore

No bitter sap

No horde of fiber-glass shells culled
From the data stream

No entering

No mania or the calm
After mania

No face in the fields
Seen only from a great height

No bringer of grief

No flesh and the sound of flesh
Pleased with itself

No conditionals

No illness or sex

No notes in mud
And mist
In war

No trace showing
The quickest way back

No light caught
In the hair of the void

No predication

No as an answer to an impossible cure

No leading to a staircase
Leading to a staircase

No delicate shape of the ear

No walking among us
We who are perplexed

No depth charge

No mineral ore

No subjunctive

No mother crossing
The lake on stilts

No angel
Of death whose wings are salt

No scattering of perspective

No horses on fire

No statues built after them

No water for the open-heart surgery

No abandonment

No longer missing

No intentions

No contrariness

No colors coming alive only in rain

No hypothetical states of affairs

No forgiveness

No echoes and echoes
Through the architraves

THE ARCHITECTS

We pried doors open
To blue, domed
Rooms when we were tiny
We remember

Much rejoicing in beer gardens
The leadership
Floating above us
A big, loud sun machine

Over sheep meadows
Now with glass and steel
We toy with our reflections
Mirroring our internal divisions

We collect and leave
Brochures in rooms for the rain
And run to the woods
With our prayer partners

After the unspeakable
We designed
A transparent ringing carapace
To descend over our citizens

Glassing in the city
So our laughter
Will always bounce back down to us
Everyday we siphon

Hymns from each other
Where we could not let go
Of the faces we have lost
There leaks heaven

THE REUNIFICATION OF THE BODY

Stay down beside your confirmation number
And be someone's garden

The orders of magnitude will mount
      And thunder past us

This is the part

When you put everything away
      Where no one can tell

The difference between the wind
And a human being

      The haze has migrated to the other eye

Cracks have begun at the knees
      And green-grey wilt in the waist

      And wrists of the everlasting

Remember that you fell

When you speak again

      Use your wilderness
         Not your factory voice

WEATHER PATTERNS

Mud comes next
After the parade and party

The skins and surfaces we know
Are the flag's

Color secretions
We attempt to defenestrate

Ourselves of ourselves
But only pass

Blindfolded through many
Clocks and membranes of lights

We always arrive years late and stand
As brittle twigs in resin

So quiet
Pages turn above us

Barking signals our homecoming
The offspring

Of mongers of mongers
We are so close to our surroundings

We are field-like
We feed the parks

THE FOLD

God was

Horses before the barn burned down.

Expired lights at night.

A pile of books in the clearing.

Bodies the next day.

I'm on my hands and knees

Again in the scalp

Of the wheat, looking for a fold

In the fields.

The scent of heavenly spheres

On the back of the wind-borne blight.

This living hides the seam of an ingrown

Other time.

Where buildings don't collapse.

The people there

Rising from their desks

Throwing

Confetti out of windows,

Waving and smiling down at us.

INSIDE THE BRIGHT WHEEL

A lesser vehicle

INSIDE THE BRIGHT WHEEL

The city streets are long and straight
But our faces could only
Point sideways

INSIDE THE BRIGHT WHEEL

Multi-part questions remain

INSIDE THE BRIGHT WHEEL

Upon arrival
A hundred machinic embraces

VOYAGER

For want of an exterior
While the fields
And the caves of our country

Grew inverted
We kept digging
Our faces slid over our faces

Shuffled by a wild
And vivid rain
We abandoned

The huts and subdivisions of getting married
What was closest at hand
Rolled away

With a thunder
In our heads
Until distance

Made the immense sky
Convex
A more metallic

Sky against the skull of our new condition
Clawing land
Having filled our chests

With the old encyclopedic breezes
We began coughing daylight
We dwindled

Large strangers came
They fed us
And they fed us

ARM & TETHER

The city extracted from the coals.

Side by side
Steam and white walls rose.

      Veins grew long on the map.

We began as daggers
Later made neutral
Later made cogs

And yet sometimes the vehement coil
      Inside the chest catches

And cars are overturned.

The distance fills
With black smoke again.

      Naked we would bite each other's mouths.

The palm of day pressing
Down over tin rooftops.

The combined weight of dealerships
Upon the heart.

MORROW

Even laughter ages on the disc
And on my chest a many-headed
Body emerges
I reach deep inside
Myself and extract
People now living in tents
There is no end to them
They want to talk to our houses
Their wounds form a pattern
Seen from the air
When the beasts descend
They tie themselves
To the ground
And let their bodies be eaten

NTH SCENE

Dusk after dusk

Unknown unknowns

Indelible increase
In the folds
Of the eyelids

An actual and virtual
Homelessness

An opening
Onto an ever-
Fecund limit

Discounts in another climate

A river

A national day
Of lethargy

A clamp advertised
As putting calm voices inside heads

Oblivion of the jetty

Reddish salt
Upon the jetty

Cuts and asymmetries

Varying states
Of wine

Wolves
Within wolves
All the way into the atom

Bare life

Mosaic virus

Blasts of spiral

Bitter air
In old accordions

A body
Of water not site-specific

Wounds of the mouth

Wounds of the tongue

Self-immolations

Blocks of doubt
And difficult time

A hypnotic
Rhythm of protests
In the pre-dawn hours

Stoppages and flows

My fellow somnambulists

POST

Sleep in your new name
Sing a little
To loosen the rope
Fix your eyes to formal
Joy before the disc skips
Have you left
Instructions for when the sea breeze visits you
Now break your gaze
The night is not completely blind
Your anger swift
And married to a man
This is no longer the Babylon
You remember, love, and gag on
How rude is the sun
Its trumpets blaring down
While citizens speed along
On motorcycles made of ash
The wind will undo the rest of us
Our gangs of dust obsessed
With the backs of our own heads
Where do the graveyards begin
How long and elastic
Is the century's atrocities' leash
Blessed forgetting be and sincerely
Your angel with the face of a machine

INSIDE THE BRIGHT WHEEL

An image of our mother
Athletically drying her hair
Fades though we attend to the image
In three dimensions

INSIDE THE BRIGHT WHEEL

Are marks on a body consistent
With a struggle and a long fall

INSIDE THE BRIGHT WHEEL

Bearded prophets side by side
Snoozing

INSIDE THE BRIGHT WHEEL

Rotundas as panopticons
Where sure
Rapid movement
Is a kind of uniform

DIVIDER

How moving
Away from pure sound
We fade into our ox and plow
Such a fever in our new
And perplexing life
The roads
And our lungs are bad
Finitude splices
Each of us to each of us
In the many shops
All closing at this hour
Tomorrow will be discounted
And another translucent
Layer will be revealed
To be viewed
From different towers
And yet will we finally lose our edges
In rows we are still
Suspended by our cameras
The background runs through us
We speak
To our photo-objects
We must mass-produce
Mirrors to stay what we are

SHELTER

One hand did glissandos
While the other

Skinned the pulsating cosmos
And pushed our heads

Back beneath veils
To escape and breathe

Clear air
Some of us grew beards

We let out call-notes
Whose crescendos the glass-and-steel

Arcades threw down crumpled
Our eidolons mongered

Random wars while our flesh
Did household chores

The decade leapt
Through curtains of wet newsprint

Squatted down
Over our pink tonsures

And expelled
A child-dictator in debris fields

It was then we freed
The archives before we became

Recorders for the rain
For all tents we provided

Backwards guitars
Inoculations coming and going

In places of worship
We made space for aleatory

Sub-committees
Asking officials not what

Boxes are for
But what boxes

Are about
We swapped out

Faces for facializations
In a swarm our closest friends

Were oblique
And everywhere in approaching

GLORY

The curtains spoke and emitted
Cries but not the birds
You said you would
Send through my wounds
To alight on electroplated
Nipa huts
The son
Of an Apega
I bring the noise up to my face
Though the sound grows
Weaker by the suburb
The cello-driven sleepless
Stagger toward rivers
Where they will link arms and float
The sweet lord has many
Moving parts said my sensors
My other job
Became branches

MORROW

If I knit you to the crowd
Would our hearts

       And groins be blurred

Our torsos
Stamped on rainwater

Our network
Of friends   sniffing glue

Asking are we being good

       Is it burning there

Are those fancy
Chairs still   being used

INSIDE THE BRIGHT WHEEL

Arranged on spears are the cakes and lambs
We let decay
To remind us of the peeling
Edges of our time

INSIDE THE BRIGHT WHEEL

A weekly idiot plays obscene
Variations on the rommel pot

INSIDE THE BRIGHT WHEEL

The washing away
Of wrongs

INSIDE THE BRIGHT WHEEL

We laugh
When we don't understand
What we say to each other

SEA OF TEARS

An ethical relation among things

      He was completely gone

The Absolute

Propped up by a broomstick
      To make us weep

As bits

      Of philosophers in the brain

Glass and blood in wool
      When eyes spill out

Here

      Please help us eat

SATURDAY GROUP

Our spleens are normal
In size

Rejoicing and the papayas
Are in bloom now

This is the work
That work begat

With knives and brushes
We are many wings

Against a chalky ceiling
Long ago our judges sank

We have a desire
To always have freedom without memory

So no one knows for sure
Who shot the mirrors

Music is fed to us
We who also drink

The milk from our elders' eyes
Our legs are strong and bright

Though we can't dance at the inside
Of a memorial anymore

We have found that mercy
Stops the heart

FLOWERS OF GLASS

Collect this null-transfixed
        Head of mine

Out of these arms

        Dear dead dog, go

Fetch me quick a green
Branch from the abyss

Meanwhile you out there
        May or may not

Be my son

As stones want
        To be stones and

Tigers, tigers

Will rings and coins
Fall through cages

Nowhere is the outcome
        Written five times

If you must take my life
Spare these hands

INTERNATIONAL STYLE

We map out zones of error
West of the museum

By morning light
               We paint

        Our dead and wondrous animals

We gut our enemies
        But speak softly into them

        By force of habit

We wake up at the same moment
        United by prosthetics

        At home we experiment
With stress positions

            We load our brushes
And return to late figuration

We cater food in the abyss
Amid the violence of the incomprehensible

        We are analogues of sugar and gristle

In another life we squat
        In large locked rooms

Comparing persimmons

REVOLVER

Soon after the men
Of our church found trees
Of smoldering meats
In the backyards of our

Married daughters
One lambsman came
Pounding at our doors
To collect his payment

We gave him statuettes
Of gold and curdled milk
When our purses evaporated
There were several

Days of silence
Followed by mounting
Loss of sleep
And disappearances

Via shopping complex
At night we suffered the obstinate
Weight and heat
Of days in the blood

Of our legs
Among us a consensus was reached
Only in fever
Then radios and guitars

Burst and answers came
Without fathers
Belts became whips
And back again

We traveled so fast
We injured the caged
Animals in our chests
But in time the pain

Dissolved with the books
We left at the beach
Through the wine the dead
Murmured their absolutions

We found joy again
And feasted
Without remainder on the other
Side of the ruins

MORROW

You and I conferenced
All night
Exchanging
Cold pronouns
We slid the glass boxes
Of our foreheads together
And then immersed
Our forearms in lard
To shake hands inside a dollhouse
We wanted to vanish
Into the structure or else
No one gets paid
We wanted to record
The rain faithfully
We photographed falling milk
We then bequeathed to still-sleeping
Neighbors negatives

INSIDE THE BRIGHT WHEEL

Owners tether
Their zeroes down

INSIDE THE BRIGHT WHEEL

We drift in and out of our skulls
On the streets
Petting the dogs of small delights

INSIDE THE BRIGHT WHEEL

The truly blessed return as stillborns

INSIDE THE BRIGHT WHEEL

The poor are still the poor

INTERHUMAN

Paradise leaked and the system
Experienced a series of convulsions

On conveyor belts
We improvised our proteins
And dubbed it continuous dining

We formed small groups

We gave ourselves to each other
There on the beaches

Every time sorrow
Circled and bit us
We administered miraculin

Our bellies filled with dull ringing
Reminding us of our successes
And failures with rice

Our nights were states of inaction

But we rustled when we worked
Side by side on the factory floor
Interrupted only by sudden birth cries

We forgave each other
Our not dancing

We were very good with absence

When our world ended
We were not changed

THE WALK

Dissembling at the podium
But spectacular in bed.
What was the last
Question again?
Yes, my stabs
Have healed.
I've taped the box
To this bad self.
Thursdays are wrong.
And breathing takes
Time. I tripped on the map
After I followed the stubborn
Thought to the park.
Around here it's all about
Organization.
An icy room with cows
Dangling inside it.
We're sorry we missed
Your business by a few burning
Towns. There is water
On "always."
The wind still roped
To a tree.
Clavicle, wind-handle, I want you
To treat me like work.
Don't ever stop. Days
Zoom right through us.
Until the mob and truth
Of these places
Strip us of our cameras.

TRACE EVIDENCE

The house repeats itself
In the hammer blows
At the wound-site
Where the sky
Is still bruised above the radio tower
Long ago destroyed by narcoleptics
And when the curtain parts its lips
It is only the empty morning stuttering
Tapping on the pane
With a branch
Having forgotten its keys
We think how stupid of it
But our skulls are on the outside
When we run and finally disappear
Our families keep recording

MORROW

In the clearing
In the fragrant heat
I ran my fingers

Through my beloved's
Hair checking
For lice and daymares

But our bed of leaves disguised
A complex network of gears
A whole abysmal

Marketplace
I lost all
Feeling in later systems

The epoch a muscle
Stopping twice
Bittersweetness

Was a year in June
Over the countryside
The great wheel

Spun
With the helicoptering
Angels

Our souls were scattered
Only half of us
Sang

HOSPITALISM

Though its surface feels like a gurney
An eroding kiss

Smoke in our hair
Let's consider when and where

The gilded painting's been
Beneath the weave

The gauzy blue
Of receding labyrinths

Leads to the last day of fever
One moth

Leaps and we fall
Down from our fathers

This real
Life in curtains

And on the screen
A beautiful aneurysm

A rose
Burns for example

And fear of parks
Never because longing and sidewalks

After rain
Unmoor vapor ships

But the simple fact of the moon
Lowering its destroyed

Engine on chains
Someone please explain

Why the ballad keeps breaking off
Mid-sternum

The growing presence
Of photographs on our necks and arms

A grace not achieved in life
Is Technicolor

The gaze spills
Past the tracking shot

And swerves
To the window at the end of the hallway

To the bottom of the stairs
Where we suddenly

Wake up on our knees
Still praying

INSIDE THE BRIGHT WHEEL

Is non-action
The windows are painterly
Abstractions

INSIDE THE BRIGHT WHEEL

The departed
With their incomplete absence
Exhort us not to let go
Of children and music

INSIDE THE BRIGHT WHEEL

Cavort musical automatons

INSIDE THE BRIGHT WHEEL

New birds do not fly
But roll like spindles

BROWNFIELD

Hands descend
        Hairs and fevers

             Descend
   Meats

   Descend

Voices and likenesses descend

Our husbands also descend
        Where goodness is made to wait

        And kneel at the water's edge
And we are drunk on their resemblances

Our dead are so naked
And awkward in their graves

       We could not winter in their names

We dissolved home
Daylight gave us heat

And then stopped working
       We fell into grief

       Because lights in buildings
Now separate us

To cry is to start thinking
       To point at one's belly

And then point at one's bleeding
       Mouth is to begin the mute harvest

We lurch forward
We breed for speed

       And forgetfulness

Knowing staying will only metastasize
       To a lingering disease

Animals and plants surrender us
       Their dreams in their passing

We are persons full of stones

All we are
       Are our papers

NOIR

You believe you are in the world
Without example

You stay with your vehicle

Your sleep
Leaves no trace

You tourniquet
Around a phantom limb
The time of your home country

You tattoo
Your anniversary to an acoustical
Membrane over an abyss

Your voice and all its qualities
Drop in place

So when you yelp or mumble you are mindful
Not to invert yourself

You take a detour
To examine your neck and face

Bending you assign
Tactile values
To terrifying objects

You think hollowness unlike depth
Is a grace or a loveliness

You stretch your skin
And let a film play all over it

THE KINGDOM

Neo-animals we
Slept with our veterinarian
Nightlong his face
Was the nearest

Grey object
And later in the daylight
We walked until a wall
Inward and dishonest

Completely gave
On pavement we
Joined shadows
Rain plus the ground

Radiation of its complex
Odor
Memory's
Wind-sculptures

Spin funnily with leached
Colors
Above our heads
We spine-dangle

And then we
Stretch horizon-like
We are vessels
Bearing wine that floods up

From our song- and field-
Stoppered necks
Having left our names
The future drinks us

BARDO

How far have we traveled
And when did the avalanche
Of our vehicles come to a stop
On the highway in our linked loneliness
We imagine ourselves a modular
Horizontal sculpture
We reminisce and pine for the remote
Persons we made happy
To amuse ourselves as vultures
Or shards of sheet-metal roofing
Wheel overhead
We burn or trade
Official documents
Our duty now is to never say no
To anyone who points a flashlight
At our windows in the night or in the fog

MORROW

Because I have no belief
This body is a plastic
Tube where passes day
Leaves
Gummy residue
No limb of him
Logs on as me
What is rising from the couch
Contemplating the partial
Birth of my hands
In a place between one
And ten thousand
I waited amnesia ago
To lose to not
Ever find the plectrum

ADVANCES

An inch per human

Milk and white vomit

A cascade of stripes in the museum

     A rip waiting to happen
Down the turn-of-the-century dress

     Cubist injury
     Colonial

Revolt under a cloud of lenses

Comes a lull for us to weep

And bleed into our helmets

INSIDE THE BRIGHT WHEEL

Self-doubt

INSIDE THE BRIGHT WHEEL

What is the prayer count?

INSIDE THE BRIGHT WHEEL

Dear ventilated burial grounds

INSIDE THE BRIGHT WHEEL

I hid my eyes from us

ALTAR PIECE

Can you hear us there
In poverty
At the back of the engine
We've grown more frail
From the date of purchase
As out of mud
The lotus rises
So a melody blooms
From the mouth of a statistician
But the sky keeps peeling
And a sudden burst
Of cold has shocked
Melismas
Now there is gagging
In the pale background
Everywhere the bright seeds
Of shrapnel rest
We share
One torch-bearing prosthesis
We march to the cliffs
Where our kids are echoic

RESTORATION

Where our eyes are blank
We fill with moths

Bony fingers of daylight flit
In and out of our faces

The farther we step
Away from our desks

The more rain and cardiac
Events escalate

Dancing on rooftops
Requires less music

And more animal
Having scattered we return

Our leaders to their plows
Our dogs upon our citizens

We are known by mirrors
We are policed by mimes

MORROW

When you're not   revolving
In the fields you're burning

        Holes in the labyrinth
Remember   this is why

We changed to appointment-
Based systems
But why   have you appeared

Today is not a Tuesday

And very early tomorrow
You must   be gone

To an engagement
Where rows of trees and statuary

Broken off at the knees
Converge   inside a lens
Looking back

You will take off your hat
And clog the vanishing point

THE STATE OF THE STATE

Tenderized
Post-citizens
We keep warm
In our blood compartments
Until antinomies
In our thinking arise
By spinning cop-light
We are found
Roaming in our sleepwear
Desiring this
Or that machine
When we start
To lose consciousness
We call out our own names

EVER

The day is dead
              The face and arm

Disappear

              Correct?

Even with pigeons pushing buttons
Or pecking at breadcrumbs

In town squares
              At church steps

              Or on factory floors

                    The disconnects are legion

Our nephews and nieces
Are no longer our songs

              We check against copies

And eat the pages
              As we read them

We absorb milk
And nothingness

              While wide, rotational
Noise defines the city limits

              And broken birds

Roll down
The hills around our houses

              The distance grows
From inside us like anesthesia

We tried
To move away once

      But we were defeated by weather

We sit
Transfixed as attendants

Wheel away the dusk and floodlights
Squeeze through the trees

      We hum

Not in pain are we

      Most alone
But in music

INSIDE THE BRIGHT WHEEL

You enter a series
Of amphibious cities

INSIDE THE BRIGHT WHEEL

The people are rolling
In the ash
When they are not
Moaning in the maze

INSIDE THE BRIGHT WHEEL

Rattles made
From the toroids
Of dried navels

INSIDE THE BRIGHT WHEEL

Not day
Not night
But sepsis

THE FUSE

Come child-bearing age
Waking up

Wounded we will leave
The corn maze

For the actual horizon
And while we still dream of an ethics

Hallucinate another day
Stroll through an installation

Of bones and white buildings
To be demolished completely

But remembered while driving
Because cars are an eternal river

Crammed with restless limbs
And even though our faces

Might shake
Violently in the mornings

And the twilights of the future
Soft clicks

And bright screens
In cubicles will steady them

MORROW

Until a tunnel opens
And a newly formulated
Scent leads the way
We retire with our animals
And sleep by definition
So many minutes to a field
The rush and rasp of cash
We feel for the first time
The grass is truly alive
Crowds soften
Into the soil
Wheels cut deep
Our rambling, perfumed
Automatic letters return
To our selves unread
These dreams we slowly eat
Between buildings
Under a willow-work of chains
While the wind holds
Fast to the walls
Like the drowning to the trees

ONE THOUSAND

Structures dance

     Great is the guilt
          And to burn is to burn

Lowness becomes our new heaven

     We remain calm behind a wall of horses

We build horizontal monuments

Dream enclosures

     And sleep in shifts
          In octagonal arrangements

Becoming signatories to moths

     We find our faces
          Among the disembodied

          Our eyes and mouths

     Embedded in a gelid medium

It is peacetime
     And the summer of many experiments

The tarpaulins cannot cover
     All of us

We are half people

     Half houses

THROUGH ERROR

Now is night
Seeing is excision

Our neighbor's room is a box
To make ours colder

Our nurse is a name

Where is the melody in the wine

We have gone
Very far into not eating again

There is joy and warm
Feeling without accumulation

But we must look everywhere for it

Anything that is hollow
Has a scent that lives on

A microphone empties out
Into the ribcage of the public

We believe in a face
That revolves but does not change

INSIDE THE BRIGHT WHEEL

When is the eye
Not a fist
Dilated by knives
But limited by technique

INSIDE THE BRIGHT WHEEL

A line of drunkards
Scale a row of sycamores
To praise
And elegize money

INSIDE THE BRIGHT WHEEL

The first
Few kills

INSIDE THE BRIGHT WHEEL

Amnesia

TONE/SHOCK

We sang lullabies to our neighbors
                        And then we hurt

And bored them so they would grow
                Deeper interiors

We texturized their peace
                       We fed them faith

With parts of faces
            Ours was a fatherly response

We created longing
                  Before we invented tourism

We demolished slums
            But preserved the aviaries of childhood

We were the long
                  Lawns while the muzzle

Flashes in the fields
                Were our sisters

WORK SONG

Slow hollowness
Inheres to things

We think our way
        Into a new valley

Our foreheads leak

        Fear runs the engine

And from our thinning hair radiates
        The smell of keys

We cloak ourselves
With companion devices

An evening melody
        On our lab coats

Has overstayed

Our record- and peace-
Keeping done remotely by objects

Shiny and swift
        On which their owners'

Faces are inverted

        Our money becomes

Water or rust
In larger markets

        The old crowds

Are as soft

As they are deep
In the olive

        Harvest of our hands

We will join them

MORROW

If the grid does not scar
Or coagulate
My living hand
Crawls free
If dogs fold the sheep
And I control
The cars of my neighbors
I quiet guns
If I fail
They empty
Their cupboards
Stab me
And climb into my mouth

STAGECRAFT

Now we form

Dance troupes
Now we manufacture

Needles

Now we make ourselves
Very, very small

Now our sons

Are crumpled around their instruments
Now we play captors

Now we run

Away from representation
Now softness sinks

Beneath the surfaces we rest against

Now we surrender our land
Now we play

Sports involving the ocean

Now by flares
We are singed to nakedness

Now we hide behind bags of sand

Now air flows into our masks
Now we make nice

With the wolves inside us

Now we learn
Helplessness for everyone

Now we trade warmth

For the pleasure of the group
Now we are pacified

By the breeze on our foreheads

SCROLL

Intoxication in a year

An afternoon
          A fallen tree

And ashes in common

These are the bone-quiet houses

And so we nap for good

Everyday a version of childless
          And the lake

The lake is very sweet

INSIDE THE BRIGHT WHEEL

False storefronts appear overnight
At the foot of the mountain

INSIDE THE BRIGHT WHEEL

Twilight fused to the fur
Of a dead fawn

INSIDE THE BRIGHT WHEEL

Daily truth-making

INSIDE THE BRIGHT WHEEL

The bosom of the law

THEATER OF OPERATIONS

Here comes wind crucified to a horse
And dust that was breathing once
Reconcile the columns
And the arm will be
Grafted back to you
No heroic aftertaste
Only sleep and amnesia
Forced march of night
Across the eternal eyelid
A bridge goes there and after
A decade vanishes
This camera ripens between us
Scrawled across the window pane
Symbols for eating
Days versus non-eating days
This strange wind
Trained on a wire fence
Pleases the authorities

SURFACE EFFECTS

Our marriage was yesterday
We took pictures of our food
Our slow
Eating was symbolic

We raised our wine glasses
To a soldier
Every hour being born
In the middle of the day

With muted cries and distant barking
The sea breeze
Unfastened its overcoat
Dropped a mutilated gull

And we fainted
When we came back from the syringe
The sea was no longer
The beginning of a face

The waves were much faster
Than we remembered them
A substance has leaked
Away from the community

Leaving the smell of bleach
And a dull sheen on things
We hold each other and weep
We praise the quality of the image

CIVIL TWILIGHT

Absent
Emaciated or obese

Choosing the cloth-
Mother with no milk

Negating nakedness

War-torn lovers

Sweetly
Medicated ones

The number of slip-
And-fall cases

Crypts and multi-purpose halls

Between parked cars
A woman selling flowers

Dinners with a hint of gun

MORROW

And so in the throbbing
      Calm you ascend

Through the clear glass of your youngest apprentice

While your names one by one
      Leap out the windows

      With your hair your long
Shriek goes to bed

If given half a cloak you must
      Ask for the entire surgery

That there be
      A pattern to the incision

      You speed
To the victimless tomorrow of your lost teeth

In a garden of rain and rain
      Of houses

INSIDE THE BRIGHT WHEEL

In veined light
Our prisoners' torsos
Minus electrodes
Mirror ours

INSIDE THE BRIGHT WHEEL

Washing the body we realize
There is a line of cars behind us

INSIDE THE BRIGHT WHEEL

No home or marked site

INSIDE THE BRIGHT WHEEL

The empty set

WHITEWATER

Whoever loves us also loves
Our swine and chicken troughs

Our rooms and cells
Filling with day
Defeated
Day then fog

Someone in a truck
Careening
Comes to drink

Our singing notwithstanding
What if god
In his wisdom
Were completely insane

Our bodies so clean
They're smoke

THE END, THE END

Sundays we move sideways
Mondays we are blurred and folded
Into the eternal question
Experiencing
Stabbing pains
We cry out
And our crying out reveals us
To each other and ourselves
By the long hooks
Of our fears we are suspended
In an oxygenated sensitivity
That we later drag down
Flaccid
To our cubicles
Without fellow feeling we are
Motionless on a rooftop garden
By our sorrows we are lowered
Our household objects
And our loved ones glow
But we've reached
A threshold to our amazement

FOCUS GROUP

Though from our hearts' chasms
Glissandos welled up

We were not cured of static
We became

Such alarum bells
And sirens of a stupendous animal

When the Commonwealth, bursting, finally
Expelled noxious waters

We rushed to the boats
Our bodies having made

Bridges and beds
Black lights passed over

We drank
Water from our uniforms

And tasted
The dead in everything we ate

We waited for a pattern
To cut down through the clouds

We measured our era of drifting
Not in years but daughters

THE TURN

Is this our father in the clay

A thrum of high-tension

Wires in the blood

Of days going by

Are these rooftops and domes

The sweat and breath

Of the people

Are they connected

By long tunnels

Between naps

Or between songs

Will the shootings stop

Will amnesia tomorrow be

Mixed with fat rain

And bearded absences

Should the men muttering

Over the waters

And the mourners

Be forced away

Are dogs and the infirm

Moving through ruins

As we speak

Lost souls

Necking now in model units

Who belongs

To this wounded face

How do we

Extinguish our hands

In prayer

When will the guest speaker be

Wheel-chaired into the room

To much applause

And the long

Promised calm

Arrive on wings of cops

INSIDE THE BRIGHT WHEEL

All day
We scrub and dry
Winding sheets

INSIDE THE BRIGHT WHEEL

Our work is pure
But our dreams bear fatigue

INSIDE THE BRIGHT WHEEL

Nakedness + calisthenics

INSIDE THE BRIGHT WHEEL

During coffee breaks
Or happy hours
Caress your co-workers' cheeks
Though their faces are earth
In your hands

STATE OF EMERGENCY

Crowd-drift goes
Into error

Gets
Paid on a Thursday

Assumes positional
Asphyxia

Contained within four
White horses

Sharp pills under the mattress
Tethered to the museum

The sun a yellow
Hammer let go

In the name of god
The sun again

Pissing all day in the snow
So much laughter

Thrown clear of cars
The massive days misbehave

The leaves hover
We die but we do

Not sleep
We watch and watch

For the changes
We make ten copies of the morning

MECHANICAL GARDENS

Who owns
These woods
Owns
Cold data in different rooms
A waiting car
So that we may know
The backs of others
The tops of our desks
Are mud, blood, and grass
The contract states
That shadows roll
Back into their houses
Whenever we drive by
A curfew of the skull
On the plains
Where they built us

MINISTRY OF INTERIOR

With fever
We walked backwards
Through lights in the mall
Lost kids
With binoculars
And balls of string
We traced assassinations to a row of trees
One of us was shouting sentences
Into another
One was the translator
The other, cowering, with his fists
Against his ears
Our father
We honored our night nurses
There were candles
Stares and nervous
Laughter at opposite ends of the electrocuted
Memory
Rowed back to us slowly
As we were doused and beaten
The mornings stacking
Then toppling the empties
It was the slow
Week after
The end of an idea
The knife felt
Dull after a while
When the Absolute entered the surgical field
We couldn't tell
If the parade ended or began

PARK LIFE

In auditoriums
Under perpetual construction

    We clap for absence

Our mouths are muppets

    We play tape loops in our song-pipes

    We stitch notebooks
    For all persons

In the end
We are voted most mask-like

    Here we make circles
    On the pavement

The structures all around us
Are towers

    The vast trapezoids
Once were wastelands

The central monument is a multi-tonal
    Grey slab with child

In our wisdom and benevolence we've made a hum
    Bisect the public garden

Clearing a path for the blind
    And the sleep-walking

    Our hearts have expanded
With various forms

    Of joy post-consumer
Our larger fears are theater

MORROW

Tree, I let
Be devoured by your shade
My blood and my blood's parasol
I funnel mortal laughter
Into the fruit
When to awaken is to descend
A narrow stairwell and then stand
In a tunnel of faces
In passageways for bread
At crow-rise
While shouts bloom
And drop from your branches

Tree of teargas and truncheons

Tree of wild interior rains

Tree spitting sideways into traffic

THE HIDING PLACE

There was no hiding place

Things gave birth to themselves
And were crowning in their full transparency

In their lack of embarrassment
In front of us

We were small in number and had not heard
Applause before

Although when it dissolved
We recognized it for what it was

Depth bloomed everywhere

But a many-years' descent
Through dust

Revealed the limits of its device
This is the story

Of how we now crowd
In the claustrum

And flog each other's backs

And fire rifles

At the bellies of clouds

And wait for rain to reach down the muddy walls

The sky is an oasis we will not taste

Its edges are blurred
Where the membrane of our world

Flapped

ACKNOWLEDGEMENTS

I am indebted to the editors of the following journals in which some of the poems in this collection have appeared, sometimes in different versions: *Boston Review*: "The Fold"; *Colorado Review*: "Flowers of Glass"; *Fence*: "Advances," "Breathing Exercises," "Sea of Tears"; *High Chair*: "Divider," "Hospitalism," "State of Emergency," "The Search Party," "Trace Evidence"; *Lana Turner*: "Book X," "Glory"; *Ploughshares*: "The Reunification of the Body"; and *Toad Suck Review*: "Operant Chamber," "Restoration," "The Architects," "Saturday Group," "Tone/Shock."

I am also deeply grateful for the support of Lake Forest College, Madeleine P. Plonsker, the New York Foundation for the Arts, and the Santa Fe Art Institute. Lastly, a thousand thanks to my Cornell MFA cohort, and my friends and mentors who made *Throng* possible: Poklong Anading, Chico Beltran, Louie Cordero, Alice Fulton, Manny Migriño, Jenn Morea, Kaloy Olavides, Alex Papanicolopoulos, Allan Popa and the High Chair prayer meeting group, and Jun Sabayton.

The images on the cover are from *Anonymity* by Poklong Anading.

THE MADELEINE P. PLONSKER
EMERGING WRITER'S RESIDENCY PRIZE

www.lakeforest.edu/plonsker

Yearly deadline: March 1